DANCE

STAND

RUN

STUDY GUIDE

ALSO BY JESS CONNOLLY

Dance, Stand, Run
Wild and Free (with Hayley Morgan)

DANCE STAND RUN

THE GOD-INSPIRED MOVES

OF A WOMAN ON

HOLY GROUND

STUDY GUIDE

SIX SESSIONS

Jess Connolly

Dance, Stand, Run Study Guide
Copyright © 2017 by Jess Connolly

This title is also available as a Zondervan ebook.

ISBN 978-0-310-09021-2

Requests for information should be addressed to:
Zondervan, 3900 Sparks Dr. SE, Grand Rapids, Michigan 49546

Published in association with literary agent Jenni Burke of D.C. Jacobson & Associates LLC, an Author Management Company, www.dcjacobson.com

Cover image: *Creative Market*
Interior design: *Kait Lamphere*

First Printing August 2017 / Printed in the United States of America

CONTENTS

HOW TO USE
THIS GUIDE

◆

GROUP SIZE

We are designed by our Creator to be in relationship with one another. We are designed to Dance, Stand, and Run together. This study is best experienced in a group setting. Whether that is in a home, at a church, or some comfortable gathering space does not matter. For women to gain the full benefit of the study, it is recommended that large groups break into smaller groups of four to six women each after each video teaching session for the group discussion time.

FACILITATION

Each group should appoint a facilitator who is responsible for reading the Intro, leading the Prayer Pause, starting the video, and guiding the group through the discussion exercises. It is important that each participant be allowed time to respond and share as well as maintaining a safe and open environment to get the most from this study.

Please emphasize the importance of confidentiality within the group, and encourage all participants to uphold an oath of respect, grace, and care for each member.

MATERIALS NEEDED

You will need the *Dance, Stand, Run* DVD or digital video study. Each participant should have her own *Dance, Stand, Run* study guide. Reading the accompanying chapters in the *Dance, Stand, Run* book as a part of your study experience will add valuable depth and insight and is recommended, but not required.

TIMING

The time notations of each video segment on the back of the DVD allow you to plan your group discussion time. Prior to viewing each video teaching, it is suggested spending 5 minutes for the Intro and Prayer Pause. For the most benefit, allow at least 30–45 minutes for Group Time after the video.

STUDY GUIDE

The study guide leads you through the Group Discussion and Personal Study each week. The Personal Study is divided into three parts. Each part can be done on consecutive days or however works best for your schedule. Time is intentionally left between sessions to read the companion chapters in the *Dance, Stand, Run* book.

Part One

DANCE IN GRACE

Session One

LET'S GO BACK

It's okay if we've had some misconceptions about grace, holiness, and mission. But it's time for us to go back to the beginning of our faith and sort them out.

Suggested Reading in *Dance, Stand, Run*:

INTRO, CHAPTER 1

INTRO

(To be read by facilitator)

Ladies, friends, sisters: are you ready? This week, we're not going to ease in gently but jump in with both feet and get started. We believe that Jesus went all the way to the cross for us, so let's follow His lead and go all the way to an honest place with ourselves and one another.

This first session is called "Let's Go Back," and it's going to be a gospel-filled refresher about who God is, who we are, and how we're meant to relate to Him. While we'll be covering some basic tenets of our faith, you might find you don't have such basic and straightforward feelings toward these principles. Thank goodness that this group is a safe place where you can process, repent, shift, and go forward in grace. Let's go.

PRAYER PAUSE

Take a minute now before you begin the video and ask God for the boldness to go confidently into the throne room of grace (Hebrews 4:16), and thank Him that He gives wisdom generously without finding fault in us for needing it (James 1:5).

WATCH VIDEO TEACHING, SESSION 1 (17 minutes)

Use the space on the following pages to respond to some of these questions and statements as you hear them in the video. Don't worry about the right answers; go for the honest ones.

Video Notes

Who is God, and what are we here for?

Have you ever tried to hide your holiness?

2 Timothy 1:7 says we've been given a spirit of power, love, and self-discipline. Which, if any, of those are difficult for you to believe you've been given?

What *is* holiness, anyway?

What is God's stance toward us?

What are we here for?

GROUP TIME

Divide into small groups if you have not done so already. It's your turn to answer some questions and let the Lord start to change the world via your vulnerability and community with one another.

Open Up

Take 10–12 minutes to share your answers to the questions Jess asked her friends in the video.

What do **you** picture when you worship? Where is your mind? What do you see or what are you thinking about? Literally, no answer is a wrong answer!

Grace. Holiness. Mission. Which feels the most familiar and easy to understand? Which, if any, of those topics feels tender or a little murky to you?

Video Quote

Select one participant to read aloud the following quote from the video.

What I've found is that we can all be the experts on grace and holiness if we're believers in Jesus. We're all covered in the same grace and given the same image-bearing identity. Who would you count as the expert on going to the moon—the guy who has read the most books about it or the guy who has actually gone there?

Read God's Word Aloud Together

Therefore, since we have been justified through faith, we have peace with God through our Lord Jesus Christ, through whom we have gained access by faith into this grace in which we now stand. And we boast in the hope of the glory of God. Not only so, but we also glory in our sufferings, because we know that suffering produces perseverance; perseverance, character; and character, hope. And hope does not put us to shame, because God's love has been poured out into our hearts through the Holy Spirit, who has been given to us.

You see, at just the right time, when we were still powerless, Christ died for the ungodly. Very rarely will anyone die for a righteous person, though for a good person someone might possibly dare to die. But God demonstrates his own love for us in this: While we were still sinners, Christ died for us.

Since we have now been justified by his blood, how much more shall we be saved from God's wrath through him! For if, while we were God's enemies, we were reconciled to him through the death of his Son, how much more, having been reconciled, shall we be saved through his life! Not only is this so, but we also boast in God through our Lord Jesus Christ, through whom we have now received reconciliation.

ROMANS 5:1–11

Group Discussion

(Discussion to be led by facilitator; cover as many questions as time permits.)

1. Using the Romans 5 passage, take some time as a group to list 4–6 observations of what is true about us and what is true about God.

2. Compare the observations you made about God's truth to your own personal perceptions of how you relate to God and how He relates to you. What is different? What is the same? (If you can, use the answer you gave earlier about how you picture worship.)

3. This week's video teaching took us back to some basic tenets of our faith that are easy to minimize as elementary or inessential since they are so countercultural to our current world. Let's just start with these three:

   ✦ God is continually leaning in with His grace because we are continually needing it.
   ✦ God has made us holy because we're made in His image.
   ✦ God has given us one clear mission on earth: to make other disciples of Jesus.

   Discuss these truths with one another, identifying what the Romans 5 passage says about our relationship with God and what that means for each of us personally. (If you'd like to consider a few other passages, use these: Matthew 28:19; 2 Timothy 1:9; 1 Peter 2:9.)

4. On a scale of 1–10 (10 being easiest), rate how easy it is to believe the following statement: *I am already holy because of who God says I am, and I belong exactly where I am because I belong to the kingdom of God.*

1   2   3   4   5   6   7   8   9   10

Share your ranking and why with the group.

Take a minute and share how you think your life would look differently if you believed that declaration with your whole heart, your whole mind, and your whole life.

Let's Move

(To be read by facilitator)

We are not a people called only to pondering. We are women who've been set free and have been given a commissioning to *run* on mission. Each session we are going to encourage one another in a little project—some sort of action step we can take to live out what we're learning. It's incredibly important that we remember these God-inspired moves are our privilege and our get-to, not something we have to do. Report back to one another about how your project goes the next time you meet. Check in with each other while you're apart (by text, email, or drop by your friend's house to encourage her). This session's project is on the next page.

Session 1 Let's Move Project

Take some time and go back to the beginning with God. Remember the story of when you met Him, what drew you to Him, what it felt like, and how He changed you. Whether it was thirty years ago or three months ago, describe what it was like when you first experienced His grace.

You could chart it out on a timeline or write a little story. You could make a video sharing your testimony or make a piece of art that reflects how you felt. Whatever it looks like for you to take time to remember and recount that season, do it—even if it just entails laying on the ground and thinking for a few moments.

A bit of space has been provided here, but definitely feel free to use separate space that allows for more room or creativity.

The Anthem

So much of what we're covering in this study has the potential to feel basic or elementary, but we know better, don't we, friends? We know that going back to the simple gospel frees us up to experience the extravagant grace that gets choked out by our day-to-day lives. We know that reminding one another we stand on holy ground is sacred stuff, and it changes how we live and interact with those around us. We also know that running on mission is the one thing we were put on earth to do and that it's worth taking our time to learn more about that calling, so we can do it in an effective way that changes not just our own world but eternity.

I'm preaching to the choir, but I do that for one reason only: to get us to sing!

End each week of your time together by reading the anthem of *Dance, Stand, Run*. You don't *really* have to sing it—that might be weird—and you don't even have to read it in unison unless you want to. But definitely take turns reading these words over your group each week and send one another out in this truth-filled declaration:

We are the daughters of God. We delight and dance in God's grace,
and we don't want to take it for granted. We've been found out,
found needing Him, and we won't go back into hiding again.

We are the daughters of God, and we stand firm on holy ground.
We didn't get here by merit. We were bought and brought by the blood of
Jesus. Here we stand, and here we'll stay. Our positioning and proximity
to God mean something, and both invite direction over our daily lives
and decisions. We are here on purpose, a part of the world, set apart to
be used by God to bring change. We don't conform to our environment
or seek its approval. We spiritually grow while our bodies groan, and
we live in this now-and-not-yet reality as saints in a fallen world.

We are the daughters of God; we are compelled by His grace and held by
His holiness imputed to us through Jesus. We don't soak up the abundance
of intimacy with God mindlessly, but we grab hold of all He has to
offer us so we can give it away to everyone else. We run on mission,
because when you hold the keys to light and life, you don't hide them.

(cont.)

We are the daughters of God, and we are ready to dance,
stand, and run in faith for His glory and our good.

Close

Review the Let's Move Project for this week, pray, and dismiss.

PERSONAL STUDY

◆

Session One

PART 1

Intro

You're going to hear it now too.

You'll hear it in worship songs and prayers. You'll hear it in the voice of your friends, and you'll hear it in sermons. There's an incredibly faint whisper of a work-for-it gospel that has woven its way into our thinking, and once you hear it, you'll begin to perceive it everywhere.

The fact is that if we've accepted the grace of Jesus by having faith in Him, then we're made holy. According to Scripture, it's black and white, as if a switch has been flipped and we've been made saints—called holy—redeemed, rescued, and restored back to who we were made to be. And yet? That idea gets less airtime than the slight whisper of work that has migrated its way into our hearts.

And it's natural! It's not that we want to believe lies, and it's certainly not that we want to speak them to one another, but these little mistruths sneak into our hearts and lives and take root nonetheless. We may even have heard them so often that we mistake them for Scripture; Lord knows I've done that so many times! I'm going to list a few (see next page); circle any that you've heard, believed, or shared yourself.

"Grace has its limits!"

"God helps those who help themselves!"

"She has the purest heart."

"You've got to give yourself grace!"

"I mean, I'm no saint."

I can't help it. My ears are ultimately pricked when I hear mistruths spoken about our holy standing with God, and I'm willing to bet you hear them all the time too. When I first started to share with friends that I was writing a study about holiness, the thing that broke my heart the most was when people would respond, "Oh I'm so glad! I really want to become more holy. We all need to become more holy."

I knew what they meant, and they meant well, but it still made me want to immediately grab their sweet faces and say, "YOU'RE ALREADY HOLY! God said so!" Usually, no matter how awkward it was, I would say it anyhow, just because it's hard to let that mistruth go uncontested.

Essentially, anything that pits the grace of God against the holiness that He has written over our lives makes me cringe inwardly. But what helps me the most is knowing *why* it doesn't sit right in my soul. So this week, I'd like to build some truth in our hearts that we can encourage our own selves with as well as the people around us.

Pray

Use the space below to write a prayer to the Lord. Ask Him to make your heart soft and to keep your mind sober. Ask Him to be loud. Ask Him to do the supernatural work of binding anything the enemy would use to keep you from receiving and standing in truth.

And if you're into praying Scripture over your study, here is a verse to use this week:

I keep asking that the God of our Lord Jesus Christ, the glorious Father, may give you the Spirit of wisdom and revelation, so that you may know him better. I pray that the eyes of your heart may be enlightened in order that you may know the hope to which he has called you, the riches of his glorious inheritance in his holy people.

EPHESIANS 1:17–18

Read the Word

"I am the true vine, and my Father is the gardener. He cuts off every branch in me that bears no fruit, while every branch that does bear fruit he prunes so that it will be even more fruitful. You are already clean because of the word I have spoken to you. Remain in me, as I also remain in you. No branch can bear fruit by itself; it must remain in the vine. Neither can you bear fruit unless you remain in me.

"I am the vine; you are the branches. If you remain in me and I in you, you will bear much fruit; apart from me you can do nothing. If you do not remain in me, you are like a branch that is thrown away and withers; such branches are picked up, thrown into the fire and burned. If you remain in me and my words remain in you, ask whatever you wish, and it will be done for you. This is to my Father's glory, that you bear much fruit, showing yourselves to be my disciples.

"As the Father has loved me, so have I loved you. Now remain in my love. If you keep my commands, you will remain in my love, just as I have kept my Father's commands and remain in his love. I have told you this so that my joy may be in you and that your joy may be complete. My command is this: Love each other as I have loved you. Greater love has no one than this: to lay down one's life for one's friends. You are my friends if you do what I command. I no longer call you servants, because a servant does not know his master's business. Instead, I have called you friends, for everything that I learned from my Father I have made known to you. You did not choose me, but I chose you and appointed you so that you might go and bear fruit—fruit that will last—and so that whatever you ask in my name the Father will give you. This is my command: Love each other."

JOHN 15:1–17

Truths

There is no sliding scale determining how much grace you need or how holy you currently are.

Look up Romans 3:23. What does this verse tell us?

_____

_____

There are no verses in Scripture that talk about God's identity, His holiness, or the imputation of His righteousness being *given in varying amounts.*

Look up 1 Peter 4:10. What does this verse tell us about God's grace?

_____

_____

There are not special cases in the kingdom of God of people who need extra help. There is not a host of believers who hold more of God's affection because they sin less. *There are not **less holy** or **more holy** people.* The Bible refers to varying *forms* of grace—not varying *amounts.*

We've **all** sinned. And if by grace, we have faith, we have all been made clean because of His work, not ours.

Write a personal statement of your understanding of holiness as it is right now.

Define areas in your life where you feel less holy or more holy.

✦ Where am I hiding my holiness?

✦ Where am I pretending I am holier than I feel?

Let these thoughts remain on these pages and see how they might change in the days to come.

PART 2

Word Study and Questions

John 15 is rich, rich, rich with nuggets of truth and declarations of God's love, but I want us to dig deep into three specific verses. We'll then look at the Greek root of a few words as well as other places in the Bible where those same words are used.

"You are already clean because of the word
I have spoken to you." (John 15:3)

ALREADY: ἤδη (*édé*) – **now, already, at length**

Look up another verse that uses this word so you can get even more familiar with it; write out the phrase where the word "already" is used:

Luke 11:7

_____

_____

In this verse, you'll see that the evening has *already come*. It's not twilight. It's not dusk. Nighttime is certain.

In Luke 11, the door is *shut*. Already shut, in fact. Not in the process of being closed, not slightly ajar; the door is closed.

"Already," *édé*, is not an in-process word. It's a completed word. Look up and record one more use of it:

Luke 12:49

_____

_____

This one is impactful because it's Jesus telling us something He wishes were already happening. So, we know for sure that Jesus is not scared of making a black-and-white distinction between things that are going to happen and things that will eventually happen.

What He's telling us is that the words that follow "already" in John 15 are already *real*. They're already *truth*. So let's look at what He says is real and true:

CLEAN: καθαρός (*katharos*) – **pure, clean, unstained**

Let's see where else in the New Testament these words are used. Write these verses:

Matthew 5:8

_____

_____

1 Timothy 1:5

_____

_____

In both of these verses the Greek word for "clean" is translated as "pure," but it's the same word. Did anyone do a "Thank You, Jesus" praise dance after reading Matthew 5:8 in light of John 15:3?

I've always read that verse of the Beatitudes and thought, *I'm disqualified; I'm not pure of heart!* But when paired with Jesus's word about our hearts *already* being made clean, I awaken to the *truth* and *reality* that I am *included*! You are too!

What changes as you realize that you are capable of the commissioning command of this passage, all because Jesus says your heart is pure?

Describe what this realization relieves in your heart.

Can I send you to one more incredibly interesting usage of this particular word, "clean," in the New Testament?

Read Matthew 27:57–60 and summarize it below.

This Greek word "clean," *katharos*, is used often in the New Testament to describe our hearts, but it's rarely used to describe objects. This passage is one of those exceptions, and it's one of those connections that reminds us God does not do coincidence.

The cloth that was used to ceremonially wrap our sinless Savior was *clean*, just as His Word spoken over our lives has made our hearts. This is the picture of imputation—His righteousness, His holiness, His cleanliness has been made *ours*.

WORD: λόγος (*logos*) – **word, Word, speech, divine utterance**

This phrase, certainly as used in John 15:3, is more than just your average statement. It preeminently describes the words of Jesus, expressing the thoughts of the Father, through the power of the Holy Spirit.

Summarize the following verses that also include context about Jesus's divine utterances:

Matthew 8:8

Matthew 19:11

Having a little more context for just these three words, now rewrite the statement Jesus made in John 15:3 with a little more detail.

By the power of His death and resurrection, purity has been written over your life with authority. How does knowing that Jesus has spoken the divine word that declares you are already clean change the way you live? If this is new insight for you, how do you think the way you live will change now?

Keep studying.

"Remain in my love." (John 15:9, 10)

REMAIN: μένω (*menó*) – **to stay or wait, to abide, remain**

Although "remain" denotes some patience and stillness, it is a verb—this is *active staying.* Let's get some context for this word. Look up and summarize how this word is used in:

John 1:32

_____

_____

2 Timothy 2:13

_____

_____

What do you notice in common or underlying in Scripture where "remain"/**menó** is used?

What would it look like for you to **remain** in His love?

Sometimes it helps me to consider the opposite of what God is offering me, because I know that answer so much clearer. What would it look like for you to *not* remain in His love?

Let's break down another word here:

LOVE: ἀγάπη (*agapé*) – **preference for; benevolence, esteem, good will**

Agapé love speaks to one's *esteem* for another as well one's *preference* for another.

Mark where you'd rate God's affections or feelings toward you on the scale below, based on how you feel.

0	1	2	3	4	5	6	7	8	9	10

He puts up with
me because He
has to.

He loves me.
He esteems me.
He prefers me.

Isn't it good that we get to stand and remain on what we *know* to be true, not just what we feel?

How does it change your life and your day today knowing that the God of the universe doesn't just cover your sin, He doesn't just entertain you, and He hasn't just let you into the back door of the kingdom of God because He feels sorry for you, but that He loves you, He prefers you? Think here. Be specific. What changes knowing God **prefers** you?

One more verse to break down.

"I have called you friends." (John 15:15b)

CALLED: λέγω (*legó*) – **to call or speak of; to say, report**

This word denotes a speech that is in progress, or the naming of something. It also refers to something Jesus says or speaks.

You know the drill by now; let's look at other Scriptures to help us better understand the meaning:

2 Corinthians 12:9

_____

_____

Hebrews 13:5

_____

_____

And let's skip right to the next incredibly pertinent word in this verse. For this Greek word, I want to give you the actual letter-by-letter definition, taking a quick pause to soak in what Jesus is calling us here.

FRIEND: φίλος (*philos*) – **a friend; someone dearly loved (prized) in a personal, intimate way; a trusted confidant, held dear in a close bond of personal affection**

I realize that this particular passage of Scripture doesn't speak specifically to grace or holiness, but it is our friend, Jesus, giving us some very intentional and direct statements regarding how He feels about us and what He has called us.

The grace here is implied because Jesus knows *you*. He knows that you reside in a fallen world where you feel the effects of sin every single day. He knows that you're going to miss the mark, and He is not surprised. We are reminded that He has called us *clean* based on *His* righteousness. He is only expecting us to stand still and *remain in His love*. Then, He hits us with that final whammy: *you're my friends*. You're the prize. You're the ones I dearly love.

To understand grace, holiness, and mission, we have to build on this foundation: His love. His affection. His grace making a way for us to be called His friends.

Define what, if anything, is keeping you from dancing in this truth.

PART 3

Give, Worship, and Read

Each week we will spend the final day(s) of personal study less academically and more actively. So often we forget how to live out what we are learning; it is never intentional, it just happens that way. It's so much easier to sit around and talk about or think about how we want to change, and less easy to be changed.

So, before you meet again with your group, carve out intentional time to give, worship, and read.

The transliteration of Ephesians 4:23 "be made new" is an active and ongoing process; it means to "be being" made new. It never ends.

Let yourself be becoming something new . . . the redeemed and restored version of who God created you to be.

Give It Away

I've found that one of the easiest ways to receive a truth for myself is to give it away to someone else.

This week, I want you to: *Partner with the Lord to creatively and passionately give away the truths you've received this week to someone else.*

Act. Engage. Express.

Live Out of the Truth That You Are Already
Clean and Called Friend by His Word!

Here are some examples, but don't be scared to reach out to the women with whom you are in community to brainstorm other ideas.

+ Tell your kids about Jesus's love and friendship.
+ Use social media to share what you're learning.
+ Write a letter or an email to a friend you know is struggling.
+ Think of someone who seems lonely and could use the good news that Jesus has extended friendship to them.

Worship with Me

Each session I'll offer suggestions of some of my favorite worship songs that are applicable to what we've studied. Let yourself dance (either figuratively or physically) to these songs, however you listen to music!

+ "Simple Gospel" by United Pursuit
+ "No Longer Slaves" by Bethel Music
+ "A Little Longer" by Bethel Music
+ "How He Loves" by John Mark McMillan
+ "Good, Good Father" by HouseFires

Read

Find a quiet corner. Grab your favorite blanket. Set out your lawn chair on the deck. Make some tea. Whatever your personal reading ritual looks like, put it into practice today and read chapter 1 of *Dance, Stand, Run*. Give yourself permission to just read.

Session Two

WE'VE BEEN FOUND OUT

We need grace, which means we sin, but we get grace, which means we dance.

◆

Suggested Reading in *Dance, Stand, Run*:
CHAPTERS 2, 3

INTRO

Sin, grace, holiness. These are words we're not unfamiliar with, but they're also weighty and what we mean when we say them is incredibly important. Let's throw in a few more: repentance, atonement, righteousness. These are "theology" words, meaning that they tell us what we think about God. And when we know what we think about God, that shifts how we feel about ourselves as well as everyone with whom we interact.

There's a heaviness that comes when we start to talk about sin that I don't think we're always meant to carry. God's Word speaks *against* condemnation and shame, not in support of it—so let's go where we're safe to go, into deep waters and theological words. Let's really embrace the freedom and light that comes with being found out, being found needy, and being found as women redeemed by the blood of Jesus.

PRAYER PAUSE

Pick one person to pray for your group. Thank God that we've been found out and been found needing Jesus (Romans 3:23), and ask Him to help us collectively dance in the grace He's given us (2 Corinthians 12:9).

WATCH VIDEO TEACHING, SESSION 2 (18 minutes)

Use the space on the following page to respond to some of these questions and statements as you hear them in the video. Remember, go for the honest responses.

Video Notes

What is sin?

How would you describe God's holiness?

Describe grace, or *charis*, in your own words.

We don't grasp the fullness of grace because we don't see the fullness of

_____.

It would be easier for us to give grace away if we took time to

_____.

The more we dance in grace, the more we'll be compelled to

_____.

What if life was less about trying not to sin and more about _____ with the holy standing God has written over our lives?

We must draw a circle around only _____ when we talk about holiness.

GROUP TIME

Divide into small groups if you have not already done so.

Open Up

Take 10–12 minutes to share your answers to the questions Jess asked her friends in the video.

Why is it so hard to give grace to ourselves and others?

Why do you think, even within the church, we feel the need to hide?

Video Quote

Select one participant to read aloud the following quote from the video.

Grace is God's grand gesture to draw us close to Him, because we in our sin would not make that move on our own. Grace is the leaning in of God toward our broken state. We *need* grace because our natural state as fallen humans calls for condemnation, not closeness. We deserve punishment, but He initiates proximity.

Read God's Word Aloud Together

God raised us up . . . in order that in the coming ages he might show the incomparable riches of his grace, expressed in his kindness to us in Christ Jesus. For it is by grace you have been saved, through faith—and this is not from yourselves, it is the gift of God—not by works, so that no one can boast. For we are God's handiwork, created in Christ Jesus to do good works, which God prepared in advance for us to do.

Therefore, remember that formerly you who are Gentiles by birth and called "uncircumcised" by those who call themselves "the circumcision" (which is done in the body by human hands)—remember that at that time you were separate from Christ, excluded from citizenship in Israel and foreigners to the covenants of the promise, without hope and without God in the world. But now in Christ Jesus you who once were far away have been brought near by the blood of Christ.

EPHESIANS 2:6, 7–13

Group Discussion

(Discussion to be led by facilitator; cover as many questions as time permits.)

1. Treat the two circles below as potential pie charts. On your own, fill out one of the pie charts with what culture tells you goes into being right with God. Is it 10 percent obedience? Would church attendance be included? Fill out the second circle with the breakdown of what it takes to be saved according to Ephesians 2.

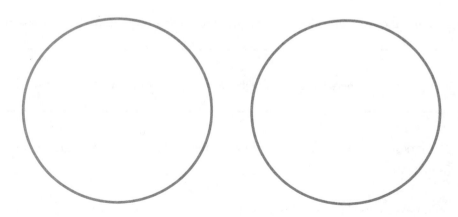

2. Discuss: What do you remember about being far from God? (Ask a few people to share their "before Jesus/after Jesus" testimonies.)

3. It seems culturally acceptable to talk about the fact that we were far from God and He saved us, but what about the continual work He does in our life? Why is it so hard to talk about the fact that He is currently covering our sin?

Make a collective list of some of the things that women in your context struggle with that feel unacceptable to admit.

4. As a group, brainstorm the answers to the equations below:

A group of women + lots of thoughts about their own sin and fallenness =
_____

A group of women + lots of thoughts about grace and how they're off the hook =
_____

A group of women + an earnest look at their own sin + an abundant view of their own grace = _____

Confess to one another sins and burdens that are outside your circle of holiness.

What are some areas where you find yourselves judging others or withholding grace? Own them by writing them down.

Now leave whatever causes you to withhold grace from others right here on the page.

Let's Move

(To be read by facilitator)

We are not a people called only to pondering; we are women who've been set free and have been given a commissioning to *run* on mission. It's incredibly important that we remember these God-inspired moves are our privilege and our *get-to,* not something we have to do.

Before reading the Session 2 Let's Move Project, ask 2–3 women to briefly share what each chose to do for her Session 1 Let's Move Project.

Session 2 Let's Move Project

Take the lavish grace you've been given and run to the streets with it. Ask God to identify one person whom you need to let off the hook. If grace is God leaning toward us to give us the favor and affection that we don't deserve and cannot earn (rather than giving us the punishment we do deserve), what would it look like for you to lean in and be the display of God's lavish love in someone else's life this week? It might be as simple as praying for them instead of inwardly railing on them in your head. It may be that God asks you to serve someone who has hurt you, or He may have you go as far as to tell them you forgive them if you've said otherwise.

Whatever you do, consult with your group to make sure others feel it's an emotionally healthy step, and then spur one another on to these good works.

The Anthem

Sing, speak, recite; one, many, all. No matter. Claim this Anthem together.

We are the daughters of God. We delight and dance in God's grace, and we don't want to take it for granted. We've been found out, found needing Him, and we won't go back into hiding again.

We are the daughters of God, and we stand firm on holy ground. We didn't get here by merit. We were bought and brought by the blood of Jesus. Here we stand, and here we'll stay. Our positioning and proximity to God mean something, and both invite direction over our daily lives and decisions. We are here on purpose, a part of the world, set apart to be used by God to bring change. We don't conform to our environment or seek its approval. We spiritually grow while our bodies groan, and we live in this now-and-not-yet reality as saints in a fallen world.

We are the daughters of God; we are compelled by His grace and held by His holiness imputed to us through Jesus. We don't soak up the abundance of intimacy with God mindlessly, but we grab hold of all He has to offer us so we can give it away to everyone else. We run on mission, because when you hold the keys to light and life, you don't hide them.

We are the daughters of God, and we are ready to dance, stand, and run in faith for His glory and our good.

Close

Review the Let's Move Project for this week, pray, and dismiss.

PERSONAL STUDY

◆

Session Two

PART 1

Intro

Things get tricky for me when I get away from Jesus. I don't mean when I get away from the church, or the Bible, or community—they are all cornerstones of my faith, and I need to continually draw back to healthy rhythms like those. But for now, I'm talking about "actual Jesus." I call Him "actual Jesus" because when I get away from spending time reading His words, I have the propensity to craft a Jesus that agrees with me or sounds like me or goes along with my plans. "Jesus in my head" is sometimes easier to understand, but he's a cheap replica of actual Jesus. Actual Jesus said some hard stuff, said some beautiful stuff, loved people well, and always wanted His Father's kingdom to prevail. He was and is magnificent, and while sometimes what He did and said was hard to understand, it was always holy and worshipful.

So, if we're going to talk about grace and holiness and even mission, let's go to actual Jesus—the source of grace, holiness, and mission—to see how it was done. The passage in John 1 that we're about to study is poetic and sweet, but the words are also astounding.

Pray

Use the space below to write a prayer to the Lord. Ask Him to give you eyes to see and ears to hear. Ask the Holy Spirit to be gentle and complete. Ask Him to do the supernatural work of binding anything the enemy would use to keep you from receiving and standing in truth.

And if you're into praying Scripture over your study, here is a verse to use this week:

"But the Advocate [Counselor], the Holy Spirit, whom the Father will send in my name, will teach you all things and will remind you of everything I have said to you."

JOHN 14:26

Read the Word

The Word became flesh and made his dwelling among us. We have seen his glory, the glory of the one and only Son, who came from the Father, full of grace and truth.

(John testified concerning him. He cried out, saying, "This is the one I spoke about when I said, 'He who comes after me has surpassed me because he was before me.'") Out of his fullness we have all received grace in place of grace already given. For the law was given through Moses; grace and truth came through Jesus Christ. No one has ever seen God, but the one and only Son, who is himself God and is in closest relationship with the Father, has made him known.

JOHN 1:14–18

Truths

The thing about actual Jesus is that He doesn't ever chill when it comes to His Father's business.

I've searched but have never found a verse where Jesus looked at the disciples and said anything similar to, "Guys, cool it. You're taking this whole worship and ministry thing too far."

No. Jesus is very clear what He thinks about worship.

Look up John 4:23–24. In your own words, what does Jesus say about true worship?

_____

_____

Actual Jesus is very clear in the **what** we are to do, but also the **how.** Write out the following two verses. Then read them consecutively as if they were one statement.

Mark 13:10

_____

Matthew 28:20b (only the last sentence)

_____

Jesus gives us the truth of what we are to do and extends Himself in grace to accomplish it. Think of a time when you have instructed someone in what to do, or a time when you had an expectation of someone (maybe a child, a coworker, an employee).

✦ Describe *how* you expected that person to accomplish your task. Did you even define the *how?* Did you even think of it as necessary?

✦ What difference does it make that Jesus says "I am with you always, to the very end" when we think of what He has asked us to do?

✦ What might our world look like if we too extended that grace—the grace of our willingness to help and intercede and stand by and go with—to those we ask or expect something of?

PART 2

Word Study and Questions

Reread: John 1:14–18.

Where do we even start with this gem? There are so many nuggets of wisdom we could explore here, but we're going to unpack just three phrases and glean all we can from them about how to put grace into action.

First, here are a few important facts to know about John, the writer of the book of John.

✦ This is John, one of Jesus's twelve disciples, and the brother of James.
✦ John also wrote 1, 2, and 3 John as well as the book of Revelation.
✦ John was a man who felt very confident in his relationship with Jesus and constantly called himself "the one whom Jesus loved," which is a pretty indicative way to self-identify.
✦ In general, John tends to be a little wordier when it comes to Jesus than the other gospels. And John tends to describe things in a more spiritual, emotional nature. Lots of talk about *logos* and light, if you get my drift.

It's hard not to love John; it's hard not to love any guy who is so sure of God's love for him. Let's dig in, shall we?

[Jesus came] full of grace and truth. (John 1:14b)

FULL: πλήρης (*plérés*) – **filled, abounding in, complete**

Here are two other verses that include the word "full":

Luke 4:1

_____

_____

Matthew 14:20

_____

_____

In the Luke passage, I love being reminded that Jesus was full of the Holy Spirit. The Father, the Son, the Spirit—they show us how community is done in the most beautiful ways. Jesus, though fully God and holy, relies on the Holy Spirit as He enters what is most definitely a trying season. If you read a little further in Luke 4, you'll find Jesus doing battle with the enemy by standing on the truth of who His Father is.

What about Matthew 14? Did you spot the word "full" there? You might have thought it would have described the satisfaction of those who ate the miraculous meal. But instead, it describes how full the baskets were after everyone had eaten.

Abounding in. Complete.

That's just like Jesus, right? When He gives what He has to give, there is not just "enough" to go around. No, He's so full, that even when He gives out, He's still abounding with all that He has. He's still completely full of stuff to give.

Write out a declaration about what this means for the grace God has given you.

GRACE: χάρις (*charis*) – **a gift or blessing; favor, gratitude, thanks, graciousness**

Ah, *charis*. Our old friend. You learned what *charis* means in your group study this week.

Write down that definition here:

I want you to look up just one reference to *charis* in the New Testament (though the word is used over 150 times). Write the entire passage below, word for word. I've got a purpose in asking you to do this, *so don't skip.*

Luke 6:32–36

_____

_____

_____

_____

_____

_____

_____

_____

_____

_____

_____

Now, everywhere your passage says "credit" or "benefit," I want you to cross it out and write *charis*.

I can't think of a passage that has more potential to debunk our broken theory that we somehow have the right to withhold grace from anyone, no matter what they've done.

And this is what Jesus comes full of—the leaning in, undeserved favor of God.

Let's hit one last word in John 1:14.

TRUTH: ἀλήθεια (*alétheia*) – reality, sincerity, truth in the moral sphere, divine truth revealed to man, straightforwardness

Oh, actual Jesus. It would be so much simpler for our minds to grasp if You were just full of grace or just full of truth. There is one camp of people who talk about You as though You were a benevolent and gentle old hippie. And it makes sense sometimes because You were so nice and so kind and so loving.

But there is another camp of people who represent You as a militant crusader, telling everyone what they did was wrong and that they were going to hell. And honestly, actual Jesus, sometimes when You got mouthy and honest, Your words weren't easy to swallow. They convict us; they mean we have to draw lines in the sand about living for You instead of living for our own pleasure.

But it seems like you were both, according to John.

Fully gracious and absolutely abounding in truth.

Can you describe a time where you felt the overwhelming grace of God?

Likewise, describe a time when God's truth has been used to sharpen, change, or correct you.

And where does Jesus coming full of grace and truth lead us?

> Out of His fullness, we have all received grace in
> place of grace already given. (John 1:16)

RECEIVED: λαμβάνω (*lambanó*) – **receive, get, take hold of**

It's worth noting that this isn't a gentle verb like the word "remain" that we studied in the last session. A deeper study into this word tells us that it means aggressively laying hold of and accepting whatever is offered. The assertiveness of the recipient is emphasized. *This is not a gentle receive; this is taking something with purpose.*

Look up two other verses that use this same translation of "received": Matthew 8:17; Matthew 10:38–39.

Now paraphrase the verses personally and claim them by filling in the blanks below.

Because Jesus aggressively took hold of my _____, I get to receive His _____ with assertiveness.

We are called to purposefully receive _____ in order to follow Jesus. When we _____ _____ _____, that's when we'll actually find it.

So, you have received grace and truth fully. How are you going to *give* it in full abundance to others?

PART 3

Give, Worship, and Read

Each week we will spend the final day(s) of personal study less academically and more actively. So often we forget how to live out what we are learning; it is never intentional, it just happens that way. It's so much easier to sit around and talk about or think about how we want to change, and less easy to be changed.

So, before you meet again with your group, carve out intentional time to give, worship, and read.

Reread Ephesians 4:23. Let yourself be becoming something new . . . the redeemed and restored version of who God created you to be.

Give It Away

I've found that one of the easiest ways to receive a truth for myself is to give it away to someone else.

This week, I want you to **creatively and passionately give away the truths you've received this week to someone else.**

Here are some ideas, but don't be afraid to brainstorm even better ways:

✦ Define grace in a poem, painting, or song.
✦ Use social media to share what you're learning about grace.
✦ Write a letter to a friend or relative that shares grace in one of two ways (say "I'm sorry" or "You're forgiven").

The sky's the limit!

Worship with Me

This week dance with the Lord to these songs:

✦ "Where the Spirit of the Lord Is" by Hillsong Live
✦ "Faithful to the End" by Bethel Music
✦ "Grace Alone" by Dustin Kensrue
✦ "Lord, I Need You" by Matt Maher
✦ "This Glorious Grace" by Austin Stone Worship

Read

This week, read chapters 2 and 3 in *Dance, Stand, Run.*

Part Two

STAND YOUR HOLY GROUND

WHY AND REALLY?

The sometimes hard part of recognizing our holiness is allowing it to permeate every area of our lives, starting with our intentions.

◆

Suggested Reading in *Dance, Stand, Run*:

CHAPTER 4

INTRO

Let's revisit where we've been so far, gals.

We've gone back to the start and remembered who God said He was to us. We've remembered what it was like when we first figured out that He was good and worthy of being trusted. We've revisited the relief and joy we experienced when it dawned on us that we're not trustworthy, but He came for us with His grace anyway.

It's becoming clear to our hearts that the joy of that grace will lose its shine if we don't keep looking at the incredible pardon He provides for our hearts. So, to see grace in its fullness, we must see our sin with clear eyes. And we're also coming to terms with the fact that it's much easier for us to aggressively receive the grace of God if we're only looking at our own sin. We have drawn circles of holiness around ourselves and we've declared, "I'm going to deal with my own junk and hope the best for others!"

But how do we actively deal with our present junk? It's all about asking ourselves some very important questions.

PRAYER PAUSE

If you haven't already, take a minute now to ask God for humility and gentleness as we tackle some tough stuff (Ephesians 4:2) and also to thank Him in advance, because I think He's about to set some daughters free from things they thought brought them happiness (Isaiah 61:1).

WATCH VIDEO TEACHING, SESSION 3 (17 minutes)

Use the space below and on the next page to respond to some of these questions and statements as you hear them in the video. Don't worry about the right answers; go for the honest ones.

Video Notes

Is there anything random you've ever become obsessed with? Any obscure thing you've questioned the purpose of?

On a scale of 1–10 (1 being "not at all" and 10 being "not a problem"), how much do you like having your motives questioned by other people?

On a scale of 1–10 (1 being "not at all" and 10 being "not a problem"), how hard would you say it is to question *your own* motives?

We are committed to agreeing with God about the holiness He has written over _____ lives, but we're not here to judge _____.

What does Psalm 84:10 say?

What does Psalm 34:8 encourage us to do?

GROUP TIME

Divide into small groups if you have not done so already.

Open Up

Take 10–12 minutes to share your answers to the questions Jess asked her friends in the video.

What are some areas of your life where you've unexpectedly found worship and honor?

Here's a little tougher question: What are some areas of your life that, though not necessarily sinful, you know are **not** actively a place where you're worshiping God?

Video Quote

Select one participant to read aloud the following quote from the video.

I think that asking "why" and "really" is so important because there's more for us on this earth than subsistent living—filling up on what culture offers us as good. I really mean that with all of my heart.

Read God's Word Aloud Together

After this, Jesus and his disciples went out into the Judean countryside, where he spent some time with them, and baptized. Now John also was baptizing at Aenon near Salim, because there was plenty of water, and people were coming and being baptized. (This was before John was put in prison.) An argument developed between some of John's disciples and a certain Jew over the matter of ceremonial washing. They came to John and said to him, "Rabbi, that man who was with you on the other side of the Jordan—the one you testified about—look, he is baptizing, and everyone is going to him."

To this John replied, "A person can receive only what is given them from heaven. You yourselves can testify that I said, 'I am not the Messiah but am sent ahead of him.' The bride belongs to the bridegroom. The friend who attends the bridegroom waits and listens for him, and is full of joy when he hears the bridegroom's voice. That joy is mine, and it is now complete. He must become greater; I must become less."

JOHN 3:22–30

Group Discussion

(Discussion to be led by facilitator; cover as many questions as time permits.)

1. This passage is about Jesus, but it's also about John the Baptist. Take a minute as a group to list what you know about John the Baptist, maybe things you can perceive from this passage but also any historical facts you already know.

2. Considering what we know about John the Baptist, or JTB, would you call his life blessed? Why or why not?

What do you think was so joyful about his life?

3. On the left side of the chart below, list what you consider representations of blessing today. Don't hold back. Give real answers of what you look at and say, "Whoa! She's blessed!" Then, on the right side of the chart, briefly say *why* you consider this a blessing. Two examples have been provided to get you started.

Representative Blessing	Assumed Blessing
Ex.: Nice house	They have stuff, must have money
Ex.: Good career	They're smart!

Stating the *why* behind some of the things we seek always sounds a little hollow and silly, right? As we say it out loud, we realize that things or experiences aren't necessarily blessings. People are not necessarily blessed because they have a nice job or get to go on vacation or because their life looks simple from the outside.

We know that (a) those assumptions aren't necessarily fair, and (b) that's not all there is to life. So many experience abundance and joy in small houses and hospital rooms. I bet someone in your group has experienced grace and the glory of God when she was at the end of her rope.

4. With this truth on the table, what things in life are you chasing or participating in that you know ultimately are hollow and will not leave you fulfilled? List them here.

5. Dream together: How would your life look differently if you honestly asked yourself *why* and *really* more often?

Let's Move

(To be read by facilitator)

We are not a people called only to pondering. We are women who've been set free and have been given a commissioning to run on mission. Each session we are going to encourage one another in a little project—some sort of action step we can take to live out what we're learning. It's incredibly important that we remember these God-inspired moves are our privilege and our get-to, not something we have to do. Report back to one another about how your project goes the next time you meet. Check in with each other while you're apart (by text, email, or drop by your friend's house to encourage her). This session's project is on the next page.

Session 3 Let's Move Project

Quit something.

I dare you. Maybe just for a week, maybe forever. It might be the 5 o'clock glass of wine that's been replacing your pursuit of peace. Maybe it's Netflix. Maybe it's the call to your sister on the way home from work, the one that you know is taking up prime, talk-to-Jesus time. Maybe it's your fifth workout of the week. The spoonful of peanut butter before bed. The subscription service that's not adding to your life but is taking from your budget.

More than inviting you to quit something, I'm inviting you to ask God what He might want you to replace with Himself. Don't quit in shame and don't feel like this is one more area for you to earn His affection. Rather, this is an invitation to partner with Him and experience His abundance more aggressively.

The Anthem

Send one another out in this truth-filled declaration:

> *We are the daughters of God. We delight and dance in God's grace,*
> *and we don't want to take it for granted. We've been found out,*
> *found needing Him, and we won't go back into hiding again.*

> *We are the daughters of God, and we stand firm on holy ground.*
> *We didn't get here by merit. We were bought and brought by the blood of*
> *Jesus. Here we stand, and here we'll stay. Our positioning and proximity*
> *to God mean something, and both invite direction over our daily lives*
> *and decisions. We are here on purpose, a part of the world, set apart to*
> *be used by God to bring change. We don't conform to our environment*
> *or seek its approval. We spiritually grow while our bodies groan, and*
> *we live in this now-and-not-yet reality as saints in a fallen world.*

We are the daughters of God; we are compelled by His grace and held by
His holiness imputed to us through Jesus. We don't soak up the abundance
of intimacy with God mindlessly, but we grab hold of all He has to
offer us so we can give it away to everyone else. We run on mission,
because when you hold the keys to light and life, you don't hide them.

We are the daughters of God, and we are ready to dance,
stand, and run in faith for His glory and our good.

Close

Review the Let's Move Project for this week, pray, and dismiss.

PERSONAL STUDY

◆

Session Three

PART 1

Intro

Don't be nervous, okay? I'm not going to get up in your grill and try to dismantle every part of your life asking "why?" and "really?" That's not my job. Besides, sister-friend, my time is full asking myself those questions!

Instead, we're going to dive into Scripture reminding ourselves *why* and *really* Jesus is the prize worth pursuing. And then *you* get to do the hard work of evaluating whether or not your actions line up with the convictions of your heart.

Pray

Use the space below to write a prayer to the Lord. Ask Him for the ability to have a pure heart and clear thoughts. Ask Him to remind you about the grace we've been studying and how much it is *for you*. Ask Him to help you feel joy as you partner with Him to live your life from an eternal perspective.

If you're into praying Scripture over your study, here is a verse to use this week:

Who may ascend the mountain of the Lord? Who may stand in his holy place? The one who has clean hands and a pure heart, who does not trust in an idol or swear by a false god.

PSALM 24:3-4

Read the Word

But whatever were gains to me I now consider loss for the sake of Christ. What is more, I consider everything a loss because of the surpassing worth of knowing Christ Jesus my Lord, for whose sake I have lost all things. I consider them garbage, that I may gain Christ and be found in him, not having a righteousness of my own that comes from the law, but that which is through faith in Christ—the righteousness that comes from God on the basis of faith. I want to know Christ—yes, to know the power of his resurrection and participation in his sufferings, becoming like him in his death, and so, somehow, attaining to the resurrection from the dead.

Not that I have already obtained all this, or have already arrived at my goal, but I press on to take hold of that for which Christ Jesus took hold of me. Brothers and sisters, I do not consider myself yet to have taken hold of it. But one thing I do: Forgetting what is behind and straining toward what is ahead, I press on toward the goal to win the prize for which God has called me heavenward in Christ Jesus.

PHILIPPIANS 3:7-14

Truths

Jesus imparts graceful wisdom about our "why" and "really" in Luke 14:28: "Suppose one of you wants to build a tower. Won't you first sit down and estimate the cost to see if you have enough money to complete it?"

Every time we question our motives with "why" and then question them again with "really?" we draw closer to living out the truth in Scripture: "Whatever you do, do it all for the glory of God" (1 Corinthians 10:31). Paul doesn't say, *some* of what you do, or in *these certain circumstances*, be sure you are bringing glory to God. No. Paul says very clearly, WHATEVER you do, be sure your "why" is to bring glory to God and when you ask yourself, "really?" you can answer a resounding *yes*.

PART 2

Word Study and Questions

Studying the Word of God. Man, may it never lose its luster for us.

I'll tell you right off the bat, friends, I'm a goal girl. Catch me at the start of a new year, and you'll find me in a coffee shop, surrounded by notebooks and calendars and asking God what He wants me to do in the coming year. On my birthday, I'm praying for a specific word or verse from Him. What I'm saying is that I like to think about where I'm going. And in this passage, there is so much truth for us regarding where we're going. Let's get started.

> I consider them garbage.
> (Philippians 3:8b)

GARBAGE: σκύβαλον (*skubalon*) – **refuse, dregs, dung, garbage**

Well, let's waste no time, shall we? Dung? Okay!

Here's something for you. This word is used once and once only in the New Testament. Apparently never again in all of Scripture was there a suitable usage for this word. It is useless.

To kick off our time in this passage, I want you to start a list (see below), declaring what is useless (garbage) in comparison to Christ for you. As you write each item, remember that this is not a meaningless list; these are bold and worshipful declarations.

If your list feels a little anemic, look up a few Bible verses that describe how the things of God are better than the things of this world.

- ✦ Psalm 118:8
- ✦ 1 John 4:4
- ✦ Psalm 19:10
- ✦ Psalm 63:3
- ✦ Isaiah 40:8

What are the areas of your life that you're just not sure about?

Your head knows that God is better, but in reality, you're just not sure. What about your spouse? Your kids? Your health? Please be very honest. What are the things in your life that, if you lost, you'd feel as if you couldn't go on?

Maybe this is the moment where you get incredibly honest about an addiction. Would it feel impossible to make it through the day without alcohol? Coffee? Social media?

There's no one but you and the Holy Spirit in your circle of holiness. Please don't be scared.

What Is Useless in Comparison to Christ for Me?		
•	•	•
•	•	•
•	•	•

Good job, girl. Now let's throw some truth on those fears.

Head to James 1:17 and fill in the blanks with me:

Every good and perfect _____ is from above, coming down from the _____ of the heavenly lights, who does not change like shifting shadows.

And one more; let's do the same for Romans 8:28.

And we know that in all things God works for the _____ of those who love him, who have been called according to his _____.

There are two life-giving questions behind "why" and "really" to ask when you take this deep dive into your heart to find where your true affections lie:

✦ Do I believe that the Giver is better than the gifts He gives?
✦ Do I trust that He knows what is good for me and is working that out?

Before we move on to the next two statements in Scripture, I want to give you some space to journal and talk out the answers to those questions with the Lord. Here's my only encouragement: try to end with some sort of declaration about *wanting* to trust Him. You don't have to falsely say that you trust Him, but you can tell Him that you sure want to.

I press on to take hold.
(Philippians 3:12b)

First, let's look at this phrase in context. Here's what the NIV says, "but I press on to take hold of that for which Christ Jesus took hold of me."

Here's how the entire verse reads in Greek.

καταλάβω **(I lay hold)** ἐφ᾽ **(of)** ᾧ **(that which)** καὶ **(also)** κατελήμφθην **(I was laid hold of)** ὑπὸ **(by)** Χριστοῦ **(Christ)** Ἰησοῦ **(Jesus).**

Specifically, consider the phrase "laid hold of."

TO LAY HOLD OF/SEIZE**: καταλαμβάνω** (*katalambanó*) **– to seize, to catch, to capture, to appropriate**

Will you rewrite that verse in your own words in light of this definition?

_____

_____

In the video from our last session, I made a bold statement about grace. Here's a reminder:

What if life is less about trying not to sin and more about
agreeing with the new identity God has given us?

I want to ask a question and give you some time to think on it today:

What if standing our holy ground is less about removing the non-worshipful things and more about laying hold of that which has already laid hold of us? Or to put it another way, what if standing our holy ground is more about remembering who God made us to be and letting our lives line up with that?

Instead of asking you to list things in your life that aren't worshipful, I'm going to ask you to genuinely detail the parts of life that MAKE YOU COME ALIVE.

Do you feel a tingle when you teach the Word? Does your heart feel light and at home when you serve the homeless? Do you go to a crazy serene place when you listen to worship music?

What, sister, has laid hold of you? And how could you do more of that?

But one thing I do: Forgetting what is behind and
straining toward what is ahead. (Philippians 3:13)

FORGETTING: ἐπιλανθάνομαι (*epilanthanomai*) – **to forget, to neglect, overlook, fail to notice**

Do you feel something building here? Can you sense a line being drawn in the sand? I believe rather than God calling a generation of women to choose grace *or* truth, God is calling us to stand firmly, claiming *both*. I believe He is waking the hearts of His daughters to take their place as ambassadors of light, life, truth, and freedom. I believe He wants to show us that He is the BEST thing on earth and that we can stop pursuing the things of this world to meet our needs.

We have all we could ever need in JESUS.

He's also asking us to stop looking to the ways we've done it in the past.

He's beckoning us to live as if our past sins and patterns of behaviors never even existed.

Answer the following question with the very first words that come to you: What do you need to leave behind?

BEHIND: ὀπίσω (*opisó*) – **back, after, behind**

Nothing too flashy here, but let's look at other places this Greek word is used. Please summarize the verses below.

Matthew 24:18

_____

_____

Matthew 16:23

_____

_____

Luke 9:62

_____

_____

Back, behind, backward is not where we want to go, amen?

Where are you going, friend? Name it.

_____

Have you determined what the prize is? Name it.

_____

What are you going to have to leave behind to get there?

_____

I want you to write the answers to those questions more thoroughly over the next few weeks, but after every question, I want you to ask yourself two quick follow up questions. I bet you can guess what they are.

Why? and Really?

PART 3

Give, Worship, and Read

Each week we will spend the final day(s) of personal study less academically and more actively. So often we forget how to live out what we are learning; it is never intentional, it just happens that way. It's so much easier to sit around and talk about or think about how we want to change, and less easy to be changed.

So, before you meet again with your group, carve out intentional time to give, worship, and read.

Let yourself be becoming something new . . . the redeemed and restored version of who God created you to be.

Give It Away

Remember, friend, one of the easiest ways to receive a truth for yourself is to give it away to someone else. This week, I want you to partner with the Lord to creatively and passionately give the truths you've received in this session to someone else.

+ Write out a mission statement about where you're going. Make it into some kind of art for your home or the background of your phone. It doesn't have to be perfect.
+ Ask for accountability regarding what you need to leave behind.
+ Ask how you can be an encouragement to others regarding what they need to leave behind.
+ You and your group are encouraged to challenge one another to find different ways to give it away this week as well. The sky's the limit!

Worship with Me

Find your headphones, put on your running shoes, close your bathroom door, roll up the windows in your car—just turn up the volume and join me in worship!

- ✦ "The More I Seek You" by Gateway Worship
- ✦ "Come to Me" by Bethel Music
- ✦ "Come Thou Fount of Every Blessing"
- ✦ "Give Me Faith" by Elevation Worship

Read

This week, read chapter 4 in *Dance, Stand, Run.*

THE PRIVILEGE IS OURS

The beautiful part of recognizing our holiness is remembering all the authority, freedom, and identity that's been given to us as ambassadors.

◆

Suggested Reading in *Dance, Stand, Run*:
CHAPTERS 5, 6, 7

INTRO

We're not going to be intimidated by fear. We're not going to respond to condemnation. We can't be tricked into thinking that God is some ominous task master in the sky who is continually disappointed with us. We are the daughters of God, and we're here to stand our holy ground.

The privilege is all ours.

PRAYER PAUSE

If you haven't already, take a minute now to ask God to help you remember the joy of your salvation (Psalm 51:12) and also to thank Him for the identity He's written collectively over your lives (1 Peter 2:9).

WATCH VIDEO TEACHING, SESSION 4 (15 minutes)

Use the space below and on the next page to respond to some of these questions and statements as you hear them in the video. Don't worry about the right answers; go for the honest ones.

Video Notes

Circle and correct what is wrong with the following sentence: *God needs us to stand our holy ground.*

Jess listed a handful of areas that holiness affords us the ability to have abundance in. Circle the ones that sound the most intriguing to your heart:

Worship   BUILDING   GIVING

Ambassadorship

Learning   Creativity

SPEAKING LIFE   BELONGING

Which of those areas have been an area of strength for you?

Is there one that you know, off the bat, has been hard for you to see as a privilege?

GROUP TIME

Divide into small groups if you have not done so already. Prepare your hearts to get real and be vulnerable with one another this week.

Open Up

Take 10–12 minutes sharing your answers to the questions Jess asked her friends in the video. Let the Lord start to change the world through you.

Do you ever feel like holiness is more about what you can't do than what you get to do? In what ways?

Name the areas of walking with God that you forget are a huge privilege.

Video Quote

Select one participant to read aloud the following quote from the video.

Not because it's good for us. Not because it's the wise thing to do. We get to commune with God because it makes us feel better. We get to commune with God, because it's in Him and through Him that we find our home. We get to talk to our Dad because He wants to talk to us, because He loved us first, and that's a privilege and an honor and a huge, massive gift for us.

Read God's Word Aloud Together

For those who are led by the Spirit of God are the children of God. The Spirit you received does not make you slaves, so that you live in fear again; rather, the Spirit you received brought about your adoption to sonship. And by him we cry, "Abba, Father." The Spirit himself testifies with our spirit that we are God's children. Now if we are children, then we are heirs—heirs of God and co-heirs with Christ, if indeed we share in his sufferings in order that we may also share in his glory.

ROMANS 8:14–17

Group Discussion

(Discussion to be led by facilitator; cover as many questions as time permits.)

1. List the different things the Romans 8 passage calls us, even if they sound a little repetitive.

2. As a group, compare and contrast the differences between a son and a slave. If it makes it easier, take it modern-day: what are the differences between someone next in line to inherit a large business and a temp worker who gets paid less than minimum wage?

Son	Slave

3. What do you suppose sharing in Christ's sufferings means? Describe what that might look like in your life.

4. Take a minute to share the fruit that you counted in the video notes. What are the areas of your life that you have seen God give you an abundant vision for what a privilege it is to walk with Him?

5. Now take a minute to encourage one another, calling out the fruit and growth you see in one another. If you've seen a sister really stretch out her place in the kingdom, tell her specifically how it's impacted you.

Let's Move

(To be read by facilitator)

We are not a people called only to pondering. We are women who've been set free and have been given a commissioning to *run* on mission. Each session we are going to encourage one another in a little project—some sort of action step we can take to live out what we're learning. It's incredibly important that we remember these God-inspired moves are our privilege and our get-to, not something we have to do. Report back to one another about how your project goes the next time you meet. Check in with each other while you're apart (by text, email, or drop by your friend's house to encourage her).

Session 4 Let's Move Project

Take one of the areas you're privileged to be able to participate in as a child of God and act on. Make a move. Take a step of obedience. If you've had a hard time with giving, just give. If you've gotten tripped up on prayer, just take a walk and talk to God. Don't over think it; you're doing it right! Take a step of obedience and encourage your friends to do the same.

The Anthem

I'm still preaching to the choir, but it's only to get you to sing.

Take turns reading these words this week and send one another out in this truth-filled declaration:

> *We are the daughters of God. We delight and dance in God's grace,*
> *and we don't want to take it for granted. We've been found out,*
> *found needing Him, and we won't go back into hiding again.*

> *We are the daughters of God, and we stand firm on holy ground.*
> *We didn't get here by merit. We were bought and brought by the blood of*
> *Jesus. Here we stand, and here we'll stay. Our positioning and proximity*
> *to God mean something, and both invite direction over our daily lives*
> *and decisions. We are here on purpose, a part of the world, set apart to*
> *be used by God to bring change. We don't conform to our environment*
> *or seek its approval. We spiritually grow while our bodies groan, and*
> *we live in this now-and-not-yet reality as saints in a fallen world.*

> *We are the daughters of God; we are compelled by His grace and held by*
> *His holiness imputed to us through Jesus. We don't soak up the abundance*
> *of intimacy with God mindlessly, but we grab hold of all He has to*

offer us so we can give it away to everyone else. We run on mission,
because when you hold the keys to light and life, you don't hide them.

We are the daughters of God, and we are ready to dance,
stand, and run in faith for His glory and our good.

Close

Review the Let's Move Project for this week, pray, and dismiss.

PERSONAL STUDY

◆

Session Four

PART 1

Intro

This week we're going to switch things up just a little and rather than studying one passage of Scripture, we'll hit three. We're specifically going to look at the privilege we have as daughters of God to pray, learn from Him, and speak life to others. If you're following along in the *Dance, Stand, Run* book, you'll know each of these topics has its own chapter.

Here's why: I believe that prayer, learning from God, and speaking life are three of the easiest ways to *immediately* agree with the holy identity God has spoken over your life. You know how people don't really get excited about a diet until they lose a few pounds? It's because they just don't *believe* themselves. Not that they don't believe in themselves, they literally know their own propensity to fail and they just don't believe they will succeed.

I think if we're being honest here (which we are, yay!), we can admit that these three areas are ones that we're "supposed" to have figured out, but it isn't happening. The assumption that these rhythms of holy identity are all basic and we've got them covered is leading us to a lack of abundance. So, let's stop assuming and start moving. We are the holy women of God and these are the God-inspired moves of women set apart.

Pray

Use the space below to write a prayer to the Lord. Ask Him for the ability to help you see your holiness as a get-to and not a have-to. Ask Him for joy and clarity as you agree with the identity He has written over your life.

If you practice praying over your study each week, here is a verse for this week:

But you are a chosen generation, a royal priesthood, a holy nation, God's special possession, that you may declare the praises of him who called you out of darkness into his wonderful light.

1 PETER 2:9

Read the Word

Let us then approach God's throne of grace with confidence, so that we may receive mercy and find grace to help us in our time of need.

HEBREWS 4:16

Your word is a lamp for my feet, a light on my path.

PSALM 119:105

"A good man brings good things out of the good stored up in his heart, and an evil man brings evil things out of the evil stored up in his heart. For the mouth speaks what the heart is full of."

LUKE 6:45

Truths

Serving the Lord is a privilege. Like being asked to dine with a king or attend a royal gala. Simply being on the short list of invites is enough to make your heart swell. But this short list is an invite to eternity. That's huge. Really something.

God knows your name. He put you on His list. He signed you up for everything He has to offer.

He trusts you, and He believes you are worthy of His promises.

PART 2

Word Study and Questions

> Let us then approach God's throne of grace with
> confidence, so that we may receive mercy and find grace
> to help us in our time of need. (Hebrews 4:16)

There aren't many verses I love more than Hebrews 4:16. Let's see what the Father might have for us as we take a closer look at it.

First, let's look at the verses just before so we have some context about what is being said. We haven't done this so far in the study, but I'd like to share them from *The Message* paraphrase. If you'd like to look up the passage in a different translation, feel free to do that as well, but I want you to hear the message behind these words loud and clear.

Now that we know what we have—Jesus, this great High Priest with ready access to God—let's not let it slip through our fingers. We don't have a priest who is out of touch with our reality. He's been through weakness and testing, experienced it all—all but the sin.

HEBREWS 4:14–15 MSG

Will you unpack these two verses even further? Write them below in your own words.

_____

_____

_____

_____

Okay, now let's head into Hebrews 4:16.

CONFIDENCE: παρρησία (*parrésia*) – **freedom; confidence; openness, especially in speech; boldness**

Before I add any thoughts, why don't you look up the following passages where this word is also used.

John 18:20

_____

_____

2 Corinthians 3:12

_____

_____

Take note of anything in particular that stands out to you.

Have you heard that quote attributed to St. Francis of Assisi, "Preach the gospel and, if necessary, use words"? I honestly think I could have recited that quotation before I ever knew any Scripture; that's how often I heard it growing up.

Did you know that no one can actually prove St. Francis said it? There are lots of beautiful quotes definitively attributed to him—wise ones about holiness and passion and not losing the fervor of our faith. But that actual line? No one is sure he said it.

And what's interesting to me is that it has the capacity to almost numb us in our speech;

it teaches us that we can preach the gospel without using words, which is actually pretty hard. We can show the love of God by serving without using words. We can demonstrate the generosity of God without using words. But the gospel? That's pretty complex.

Peter tells us (1 Peter 1:12) that even the angels wished they could grasp the depth of the gospel: this heavy and miraculous bad news that we won't make it without Jesus and the good news that we don't have to.

It's hard to be bold with our words talking *about* God, but goodness gracious, it shouldn't be hard to be bold when we're talking *to* Him.

THIS IS WHAT WE WERE MADE TO DO.

I'm going to ask a series of simple yes/no questions and I want you to be super honest in your answers. Go!

Do I believe I need to use better vocabulary when I talk to God? _____

Why or why not?

Do I need to use a different voice? A softer one? A higher-pitched one?
A sweet mumbled one? _____

Why or why not?

Do I need to be careful about what I say? _____

Why or why not?

Do I need to get my heart right before I talk to Him? _____

Why or why not?

Is it possible I will be too much for Him? _____

If so, in what ways?

Now read all three verses of Hebrews 4:14–16 together.

After reading them all together, **how** do you think you could talk to God?

Now that we know **how** we get to talk to God and **what** we'll talk to Him about, the question is **when** do we do it. I'm going to list some potential times for communing with the King of kings; you circle a few that work for you, and then star some that you'd like to try.

Doing makeup   *Before I read the Bible*

BEFORE I EAT A MEAL ALONE

AS I'M WORKING

DRIVING IN THE CAR

Using the bathroom

Before having sex   In the shower

With a friend at a coffee date

Washing the dishes   WHILE EXERCISING

Let's examine one more word in this verse.

COMPASSION: ἔλεος (*eleos*) – **pity, mercy, compassion**

Look up and write out these verses where we also find this word used:

Luke 1:50

_____

_____

Titus 3:5

_____

_____

This is such an important word because it's all about God's stance toward us when we come to Him boldly and confidently, covered in the blood of Jesus.

It's mercy. It's always mercy. Never anger. Never annoyance. Never frustration. Always mercy.

And if the God of the universe is waiting for you to come and talk to Him, filled with compassion, mercy, and understanding, can you think of any reason not to go?

> Your Word is a lamp for my feet, a light on my path.
> (Psalm 119:105)

Guys! We should all take a moment! This is our first Hebrew word study! Woohoo, Old Testament lovers, we got one!

LAMP: נֵר (*ner*) – **this word literally means lamp!**

Nothing too thrilling here. But I want you to look up one other reference where this word is used.

Write out 1 Kings 11:35–36.

_____

_____

_____

_____

Without getting too deep into OT history, any guesses about the identity of the lamp that is mentioned? The one that would come out of David's tribe? Flip to John 7:42.

Before studying this passage today, what did you think God was referring to in Psalm 119:105. The Bible, right? Feel free to say no. But the Bible is what most people think of, right? Well, I agree. But let's remember what we've learned about actual Jesus and what happens when we look at what He really did and said.

And what did John call Jesus, when He wasn't busy calling Him his bestie?

That's right. Logos. The Word.

In the space below, I want you to list every book, program, conference, product, or self-help product that you can think of that promises to help people figure their life out. Just take a minute or two and list every one you can recall.

Now, knowing what we know about Jesus being the lamp, the One to literally light the Way, and having full knowledge that we can find Him in the Word—the wisdom miraculously given to us—inspired by God for us to know Him better . . .

What would **you** suggest people do if they're trying to find the right way to do life?

If you knew all the answers to life, the actual Lamp that will point our feet where they should go, resided in one book, what would you do with it?

"For the mouth speaks what the heart is full of."
(Luke 6:45b)

SPEAKS: λαλέω (*laleó*) – **to use words in order to declare one's mind and disclose one's thoughts; to speak, assert; to make a sound**

FULL OF: περίσσευμα (*perisseuma*) – **abundance, overflow**

Greek words again. And check out another verse where we find the word "full":

Mark 8:8

_____

_____

Whoa, whoa, whoa. We've seen this before right. Slightly different word, same meaning that we studied in session 2. We read the Matthew version of this story, about the overflowing full baskets *after* Jesus had fed thousands of people with a few loaves of bread. Same meaning behind the word that tells us that Jesus was full of grace *and* truth.

And now we're hearing that whatever our _____ are full of is going to spill out of our _____.

So, what are you going to put into your soul to let it overflow, and where are you going to find it?

Using the space below and the Scripture we've already covered in this session, tell me where you'd go to let God fill you up. Even use knowledge He's given you outside of this study, please!

I think regarding all three of these passages, there is an opportunity in front of us.

Do you want communion with God? Do you want to talk with bold freedom and be met with grace and mercy?

Circle   YES or NO

Do you want a lamp to guide you on the perilous and often confusing path of life? Do you want that light to be Jesus and the Word of God that has been made ready and available to you at all times?

Circle   YES or NO

Do you want to fill your soul to overflowing with Him? Do you want to take all you can get and receive all He has to offer? Is that what you want spilling out of you?

Circle   YES or NO

If you answered yes to all of those, please write a brief purpose statement for yourself below as it pertains to the privilege you've been given as a holy woman of God. State what you're able to do and why you're going to do it. Bonus points if you throw in how it's going to impact this world for His glory.

PART 3

Give, Worship, and Read

Let yourself be becoming something new . . the redeemed and restored version of who God created you to be.

Give It Away

This week be bold. Be confident. Exercise your privilege of serving a God and King who loves you and names you holy and His.

- Invite a friend to go on a prayer walk with you. Talk out loud to God while you're together.
- Text a friend what you're learning in God's Word. Share it on social media. Hand-letter your favorite verse you've read this week. Tell your kids about your time reading the Bible and how it impacted you.
- Speak life! Encourage! Call up a friend to remind her of who God has made her to be, tell her how you're proud of the Lord in her. Tell her how you've seen Him grow her. Tell her how she's impacted you.

The sky's the limit!

Worship with Me

Serve the Lord in worship this week. Hands up or in your pockets, spinning across the floor or only in your mind. Just dance in His grace and stand firm as His own!

Check these out wherever you listen to music!

+ "Desert Song" by Hillsong United
+ "Fall Afresh" by Bethel
+ "King of My Heart" by Sarah McMillan
+ "Ever Be" by Bethel Music
+ "Sinking Deep" by Hillsong Young and Free

Read

You know how and are beginning to dance in God's grace. Now it's time to own it and stand firm on His holy ground. Read chapters 5, 6, and 7 in *Dance, Stand, Run*.

Part Three

RUN ON
MISSION

THE STRUGGLE IS REAL

Mission is our calling and it is a wild adventure,
but it's also a spiritual battle. Let's be prepared.

✦

Suggested Reading in *Dance, Stand, Run*:
CHAPTERS 8, 9

INTRO

There might be people who tell you that a life of making disciples is simple. I'd say they're not telling the whole story. There might be people who tell you that being on mission is too hard. I'd say they're not giving you a complete picture of the power you have access to. There will be people who say that the real loving thing for us to do is to leave everyone else alone and just mind our own business. I'd say they missed the part where Jesus came all the way to earth to save us from our sins, rather than leaving us be.

Mission is what we were made for. It's not simple and it's not necessarily easy, but it also wasn't meant to be a load too heavy for us to carry or a burden to great for us to bear. We were meant to walk *with* Jesus, and He has promised to do the heavy lifting. The struggle is real, friends, but the reward is unimaginable. Let's get started.

PRAYER PAUSE

If you haven't already, take a minute now to ask God for the vision to see the finish line (2 Timothy 4:7) and to remember the Great Commission we've been given from Jesus Himself (Matthew 28:18–20).

WATCH VIDEO TEACHING, SESSION 5 (17 minutes)

Use the space on the next page to respond to some of these questions and statements as you hear them in the video. Don't worry about the right answers; go for the honest ones.

Video Notes

This (mission) was a _____ idea.

Who were the first people to share the good news that Jesus had risen from the dead and that He was who He said He was?

And what did Jesus tell them to do?
  a. Go get dinner ready.
  b. Leave this serious business to the men.
  c. Go study, so their theology could be in check when they share the good news.
  d. GO TELL THE GOOD NEWS.

If mission is a marathon, at what mile are you?
  a. The starting line! I might be just starting, but I'm ready to go!
  b. Mile 3. I feel good so far, but I'm slightly fearful about what's ahead.
  c. Mile 15. I'm getting tired. This doesn't seem like the smartest thing I've ever done.
  d. Mile 20. This. Is. Hard. I do believe I'll keep going, but this is just hard.
  e. Mile 25.5. I was made for this. God said He'd help me, and He did. I can see the finish line, but I don't even really want to be done yet. I was made for this.

And let us run with perseverance the race marked out for _____, fixing our eyes on _____, the pioneer and perfecter of faith. For the _____ set before him he endured the cross, scorning its shame, and sat down at the right hand of the throne of God. (Hebrews 12:1–2)

Open Up

Take 10–12 minutes sharing your answers to the questions Jess asked her friends in the video. Let the Lord start to change the world via your vulnerability and community with one another.

If being on mission with God is a lifelong race, at what point in the race are you? How is the run going? How are you feeling?

What has surprised you about being a woman on mission? What have you learned that you didn't anticipate?

Video Quote

Select one participant to read aloud the following quote from the video.

He already won all the medals and all the awards; He actually already finished the race. We've just inherited the identity of His that invites us into this great mission, and it's our joy to get to run toward Him, bringing as many with us on the way as possible. Let's worship God and seek His kingdom, not worshiping the idea of calling or the exact invitations and giftings He may give each one of us. Let's keep the main thing the main thing. Let's keep our baggage light and let's run on mission together for the sake of our Savior.

Read God's Word Aloud Together

Finally, be strong in the Lord and in his mighty power. Put on the full armor of God, so that you can take your stand against the devil's schemes. For our struggle is not against flesh and blood, but against the rulers, against the authorities, against the powers of this dark world and against the spiritual forces of evil in the heavenly realms. Therefore put on the full armor of God, so that when the day of evil comes, you may be able to stand your ground, and after you have done everything, to stand. Stand firm then, with the belt of truth buckled around your waist, with the breastplate of righteousness in place, and with your feet fitted with the readiness that comes from the gospel of peace. In addition to all this, take up the shield of faith, with which you can extinguish all the flaming arrows of the evil one. Take the helmet of salvation and the sword of the Spirit, which is the word of God. And pray in the Spirit on all occasions with all kinds of prayers and requests. With this in mind, be alert and always keep on praying for all the Lord's people.

EPHESIANS 6:10–18

Group Discussion

(Discussion to be led by facilitator; cover as many questions as time permits.)

1. Why would it be silly to go running naked? As a group, compare that to running on mission without getting spiritually dressed.

2. Looking specifically at Ephesians 6:12 (below), define what is hard about mission, ministry, or even just standing our holy ground.

   For we are not fighting against flesh-and-blood enemies, but against evil rulers and authorities of the unseen world, against mighty powers in this dark world, and against evil spirits in the heavenly places. (NLT)

3. From the Ephesians 6:10–18 passage, circle which piece of the armor of God feels the most confusing or elusive to you, and then share your response with the group. Help each other unpack what these verses mean. (See *Dance, Stand, Run*, chapter 9 for help.)

Let's Move

(To be read by facilitator)

These God-inspired moves are our privilege and our *get-to*, not something we have to do. Report back to one another about how your project goes the next time you meet. Check in with each other while you're away—a phone call, text, or email. Or drop by your friend's house to encourage her.

Session 5 Let's Move Project

Everyone has an area of mission that feels foreign to them. Maybe it's hospitality or straight-up evangelism. Maybe you feel like you could talk about Jesus till you're blue in the face, but you have a hard time being the hands and feet of Jesus through service. Perhaps you're happy to serve in the body of Christ (serving on a church committee, working in the nursery), but you're absolutely unwilling to serve in the community or further afield. Tell God this week that you're willing to run the race in any way He's called you to, and put your money where your mouth is. Take a step of obedience, even if it's the tiniest one, toward a way He has created you and equipped you to run on mission.

The Anthem

We've been reciting this anthem for four weeks now. My hope is that these words are beginning to become your own. I'm prayerful that as you speak these words over each other this week, you take the time to listen and really hear them resounding throughout the room.

> *We are the daughters of God. We delight and dance in God's grace,*
> *and we don't want to take it for granted. We've been found out,*
> *found needing Him, and we won't go back into hiding again.*

> *We are the daughters of God, and we stand firm on holy ground.*
> *We didn't get here by merit. We were bought and brought by the blood of*
> *Jesus. Here we stand, and here we'll stay. Our positioning and proximity*
> *to God mean something, and both invite direction over our daily lives*
> *and decisions. We are here on purpose, a part of the world, set apart to*
> *be used by God to bring change. We don't conform to our environment*
> *or seek its approval. We spiritually grow while our bodies groan, and*
> *we live in this now-and-not-yet reality as saints in a fallen world.*

(cont.)

We are the daughters of God; we are compelled by His grace and held by His holiness imputed to us through Jesus. We don't soak up the abundance of intimacy with God mindlessly, but we grab hold of all He has to offer us so we can give it away to everyone else. We run on mission, because when you hold the keys to light and life, you don't hide them.

We are the daughters of God, and we are ready to dance, stand, and run in faith for His glory and our good.

Close

Review the Let's Move Project for this week, pray, and dismiss.

PERSONAL STUDY

◆

Session Five

PART 1

Intro

If the enemy gets your hope, he gets to derail your mission. And if your mission gets derailed, it's not just that you're not useful—the problem is that you forget who you are.

But! If you keep your hope centered on the author and perfecter of your faith and if you keep your eyes on the One who saved your soul *and* gave you a beautiful identity and purpose in the kingdom of God, you are literally unstoppable. No weapon formed against you will prosper; no hardship of life will take you out of the race. You will be a woman with a soul mission, propelled only by the power of God and the purpose He's given you.

We all get sidetracked from time to time, but my prayer and hope is that you have the tools you need to grab hold of Jesus with all you've got *before* the enemy of your soul comes trying to derail you. My hope is that you start running and never stop, because this is what you were created to do.

Pray

Use the space below to write a prayer to the Lord. Ask Him for the passion to keep pursuing Him with all your heart, mind, and soul. Ask Him to help you be compelled by His grace on mission and nothing else. Pray that He'd help you keep your eyes on Him alone.

If it has become your habit to do so, pray this verse over your study this week:

Either way, Christ's love controls us. Since we believe that Christ died for all, we also believe that we have all died to our old life.

2 CORINTHIANS 5:14 NLT

Read the Word

Let us hold unswervingly to the hope we profess, for he who promised is faithful. And let us consider how we may spur one another on toward love and good deeds, not giving up meeting together, as some are in the habit of doing, but encouraging one another—and all the more as you see the Day approaching.

HEBREWS 10:23–25

Truths

We're going to have to hold on tight to the hope of Jesus, and only Jesus to do mission well.

Look up Romans 5:5 and write it below.

_____

_____

Can we ever hope **too** much in Jesus? What would the consequences be of putting all our chips on Him?

Have you ever confused hope in Jesus with hope that things will all go according to your own plan? What happened?

What is the ultimate result of a life lived full of hopes for what Jesus can give us versus who Jesus is in and of Himself?

PART 2

Word Study and Questions

Let us hold unswervingly to the hope we profess. (Hebrews 10:23)

WE SHOULD HOLD FAST: κατέχω (*katechó*) – **bind, arrest, take possession of, lay hold of; to hold fast; to prevent, hinder, restrain**

Okay, hold up one second; let's do a quick refresher. In session three, we studied this word:

TO LAY HOLD OF/SEIZE: καταλαμβάνω (*katalambanó*) — **to seize, to catch, to capture, to appropriate**

These words look similar, but they're slightly different; let's break down how they're different.

"Hold fast" is the combination of two Greek words: *kata* (κατά) and *echó* (ἔχω). *Kata* speaks to proximity, closeness, even a downward motion. *Echó* is a word that means holding. So *katechó* means to HOLD IT DOWN. Keep it where it is.

The word we studied two weeks ago, *katalambanó*, is the combination of *kata* (κατέχω) and *lambanó* (λαμβάνω), which means to receive. So *katalambanó* speaks to holding on tightly, even in a downward protective motion, to something you receive. We were reading from Philippians 3 where we're encouraged to take hold of that which Christ has already taken hold of for us.

But here in Hebrews 10, we're being encouraged to KEEP HOLDING WHAT WE'VE ALREADY GOT.

Let's summarize a few other verses that use the word *katechó*, "hold fast."

Luke 8:15

_____

_____

Hebrews 10:23

_____

_____

1 Thessalonians 5:21

_____

_____

Brainstorm a few rhythms of the faith that feel incredibly important to hold fast to for you.

UNSWERVINGLY: ἀκλινής (*aklinés*) – **unbent, unyielding, resolute, firm**

This is literally the only time this word is used in the New Testament, though history tells us that it was used in many Greek secular writings. Let's break down the word the way we did the last two. It's made up of two roots: the letter *alpha* and the word *klinó*. *Klinó* means to bend, and *alpha* is used here as a negative prefix, similar to the English prefix "anti." So this translates to NO BENDING.

In your own words, rewrite what "hold fast unswervingly" means. Think how someone might get this idea across in twenty-first century lingo.

HOPE: ἐλπίς (*elpis*) – **hope, expectation, confidence**

Summarize a few other verses where we find the word "hope":

Romans 4:18

_____

_____

Romans 5:5

_____

_____

Romans 15:13

_____

_____

Circle the verse that speaks the most to you about hope.

PROFESSION/CONFESSION: ὁμολογία (*homologia*) **Greek – to speak a conclusion, a confession, or affirmation of what you believe**

Quick question: How will people know what you believe?

Do you, as a daughter of God, need to remind yourself or refresh your own affirmation often?

Is it possible to do this without words? How?

So could it be, that when we put this all together—to keep running, to keep from being derailed from the race of God—*we might need to use our words to confess what we believe so that we can hold tight with no bending?*

I think so too.

I need to be professing my faith, not only for the benefit of others, but so I can keep remembering the hope that I have. I need to talk about Jesus, not because Jesus needs me to, but because it reminds my soul where my trust is. And I can't hold fast to a confession that I'm not actually ever making, right? Let's head to the next phrase.

For he who promised is faithful. (Hebrews 10:23)

PROMISE: ἐπαγγέλλομαι (*epangellomai*) – **to promise, profess**

This word is a great reminder that God would never ask us to make professions about Him if He hadn't already made professions about us. He testified for our sake long before we ever shared our name. He prayed for us before we ever could pray to Him.

Following I've listed a few of the promises God made to us. This is definitely not an exhaustive list, just several to encourage you right where you are today. Find even more in Scriptures on your own and store them in your heart.

Jeremiah 29:11

_____

_____

Matthew 11:28–29

_____

_____

Isaiah 40:29–31

_____

_____

Philippians 4:19

_____

_____

Proverbs 1:33

_____

_____

John 14:27

_____

_____

Romans 6:23

_____

_____

> Encouraging one another—and all the more as you
> see the Day approaching. (Hebrews 10:25)

ENCOURAGING ONE ANOTHER: παρακαλέω (*parakaleó*) – **beseech, entreat, summon; to call to, to exhort or admonish**

This word is very interesting. It actually has legal undertones that paint a picture of one person standing up for another in court. This, paired with our group reading from this past week, is a great reminder that our souls do have an accuser; there is an actual being whose main intent is to tear us down and have us found guilty.

But we, as fellow fighters for the faith—as women who run together on mission—don't just offer up empty compliments or flatter one another as we encourage; we vouch for one another's souls.

In the last bit of this study, take some time to write out what kind of encouragement you could use.

First, thank God for ways you've been encouraged and admonished in the past. Was it handwritten notes? Did a friend bring a timely word just when you needed it? List those things and thank God for bringing them at the right time.

Next: get specific, be needy. What are the things you're called to, and what sort of admonishment could you use to keep going?

What practical encouragements could you use? And in what scenarios do you need prayer?

Now, *brainstorm ways you can be the encouragement that you'd most like to receive for other people.* Remember how we studied in Philippians 3 that we can take hold of that which Christ has already taken hold of in us? The same goes for encouraging others in their mission. Christ has already defended your soul and testified on your behalf to God our Father. The Holy Spirit is currently working in your heart, encouraging you and admonishing you.

What specific things can you do to encourage someone else?

Lastly, pray and ask God how you can be a culture shifter right where you are. Ask Him how you can fan the flame of mission in those around you.

PART 3

Give, Worship, and Read

Let yourself be becoming something new . . . the redeemed and restored version of who God created you to be.

Give It Away

This week, I want you to partner with the Lord to creatively and passionately give away the truths you've received this week to someone else. Don't be scared to reach out to the women you are in community with to brainstorm with one another for more ways to run on mission right where you are.

+ Write what you've learned this week and jot it on a post-it note for yourself!
+ Make a smartphone lock screen with encouragement and share it with friends!
+ Start planning who you'll gift this study to. Who might need to read or lead it next?

Worship with Me

Some songs are meant to be listened to and some are meant to be FELT. You might need headphones this week, or an empty house. It's time to turn it up and let it out, friend.

+ "Oceans" by Hillsong United
+ "Let it Happen" by United Pursuit
+ "Let It Be Jesus" by Christy Nockels
+ "Ever Be" by Bethel Music
+ "For the One" by Jenn Johnson

Read

Do you ever get apprehensive toward the end of an experience? Like you don't want to finish it because then it will be done? I do. But this experience is worth completing because it is actually just beginning. All these weeks have been training for what is to come. So find your spot. Take the time. Let yourself approach the end that is really the beginning. Read chapters 8 and 9 in *Dance, Stand, Run*.

Session Six

IN THE LIGHT, WE CAN RUN

In Christ, some of our wildest hopes and dreams of spiritual abundance can be our reality. If we seek first the kingdom, we'll have all we could ever need.

◆

Suggested Reading in *Dance, Stand, Run*:
CHAPTER 10

INTRO

Can you picture it? The women who've come before and the ones coming after us? Can you picture the ones you know now, all collected together? Your sister who lives out of state or your daughter who just got baptized? If you think hard, can you picture your neighbor, the one you've been praying will meet Jesus, in that group? Maybe your mom is there, and her mom. Maybe the woman who first told you about God. Sunday school teachers, coaches, authors you've learned from.

Ruth. The three Marys. Deborah. Martha. Sarah.

I know men will be there too, and I'm so grateful, but for now I want you to see these soft, strong, holy women of God who are in the crowd of those worshiping Jesus for eternity. I want you to picture the peace on their faces and their hands thrust upward with abandon. And in your mind's eye, if you can—get dreamy with me—look down at your feet where they stand in eternity. A little worn from running, but firmly planted where they were always meant to be: at the feet of Jesus, worshiping, and belonging.

If we know that this is our future reality and not just a dream, how does that change what we do and how we do it between now and then? And can we start to just trust some of that future reality a little more than we rely on our present circumstances? I say yes. Let's dig into our final week together.

PRAYER PAUSE

If you haven't already, take a minute now to thank God for all He's taught you as you've danced in grace, stood your holy ground, and run on mission together. Thank Him for the specific fruit He's brought about in your lives and in your relationships.

WATCH VIDEO TEACHING, SESSION 6 (19 minutes)

Video Notes

Use the space below to respond to some of these questions and statements as you hear them in the video. Don't worry about the right answers; go for the honest ones.

If we took God at His Word about His abounding grace, we'd live SO _____.

We would be so overwhelmed with the power and presence of God and His ability to transform us, that we'd be put less _____ on one another and live more _____ of Him moving.

We are *not* here to build:

We *are* here to build:

Are you ready?

GROUP TIME

Open Up

It's your turn to answer some questions and let the Lord start to change the world via your vulnerability and community with one another.

How do you think our world would look differently if the daughters of God were able to fully dance in grace, stand their holy ground, and were encouraging each other to run passionately on mission?

How can you start today?

Video Quote

Select one participant to read aloud the following quote from the video.

These women are using their hands, their feet, their voices to push back the kingdom of darkness and usher in the reign of life. It doesn't mean that they're preaching all the time and it doesn't mean they're running themselves ragged, but they are counting the call they've been given as ambassadors an honor—they're grateful to have a place at the table and a role in the work.

And the cycle goes round and round. From darkness to dancing in grace. From lost to being found on holy ground. From spinning and striving and sitting on our hands to getting up on our feet and running on mission, with the revolution beginning again and again. Each time a daughter gets baptized or a friend professes her faith. Every time a new sister's name is written in the book of life. Because these disciple makers—these holy women of God who took Him at His Word and believed what He said—know that this is what they were made to do.

Read God's Word Aloud Together

Therefore, since we are surrounded by such a great cloud of witnesses, let us throw off everything that hinders and the sin that so easily entangles. And let us run with perseverance the race marked out for us, fixing our eyes on Jesus, the pioneer and perfecter of faith. For the joy set before him he endured the cross, scorning its shame, and sat down at the right hand of the throne of God. Consider him who endured such opposition from sinners, so that you will not grow weary and lose heart.

HEBREWS 12:1–3

Group Discussion

(Discussion to be led by facilitator; cover as many questions as time permits.)

1. What do you need to throw off? What is entangling you?

2. Do you know that your particularly marked course is made just for you? Are you ready to stop comparing your path to others? Discuss.

3. What's your plan for perseverance? How will you keep running in a healthy way, as long as God will allow it? Discuss.

4. How will you continually consider Jesus? How will you keep your eyes on Him? Discuss.

Let's Move

We are not a people called only to pondering; we are women who've been set free and have been given a commissioning to *run* on mission. Each week we have challenged one another to move and each week we have allowed ourselves to be used in service to our great God. This week does not end our movement; rather it moves us to the next phase.

Session 6 Let's Move Project

Only your group knows your specific culture and the needs of your particular community. Dream up this last project TOGETHER! Ask God what it would look like to run on mission in an impactful way right where you are. Maybe you'll serve a family together; maybe you'll begin hosting mission-minded play dates. God might call you to start an event where you tell other women about Jesus, or He might commission you to pour yourselves into other leaders or women in your church. The choice is yours, but go together.

The Anthem

Your last week together. Your last time to speak these truths over one another. Take it slowly this week. Claim this anthem. You are standing on holy ground, about to run.

*We are the daughters of God. We delight and dance in God's grace,
and we don't want to take it for granted. We've been found out,
found needing Him, and we won't go back into hiding again.*

*We are the daughters of God, and we stand firm on holy ground.
We didn't get here by merit. We were bought and brought by the blood of
Jesus. Here we stand, and here we'll stay. Our positioning and proximity
to God mean something, and both invite direction over our daily lives
and decisions. We are here on purpose, a part of the world, set apart to
be used by God to bring change. We don't conform to our environment
or seek its approval. We spiritually grow while our bodies groan, and
we live in this now-and-not-yet reality as saints in a fallen world.*

*We are the daughters of God; we are compelled by His grace and held by
His holiness imputed to us through Jesus. We don't soak up the abundance
of intimacy with God mindlessly, but we grab hold of all He has to
offer us so we can give it away to everyone else. We run on mission,
because when you hold the keys to light and life, you don't hide them.*

*We are the daughters of God, and we are ready to dance,
stand, and run in faith for His glory and our good.*

Close

Review the Let's Move Project for this week, pray, and dismiss.

PERSONAL STUDY

✦

Session Six

INTRO

"My prayer is not for them alone. I pray also for those who will believe in me through their message, that all of them may be one, Father, just as you are in me and I am in you. May they also be in us so that the world may believe that you have sent me. I have given them the glory that you gave me, that they may be one as we are one—I in them and you in me—so that they may be brought to complete unity. Then the world will know that you sent me and have loved them even as you have loved me."

JESUS, IN JOHN 17:20–23

Friends, you made it!

This final personal study is a bit shorter and designed for you to reflect and prepare your heart for what's ahead. Feel free to dig back into your notes, look over your prayers, and take the time to seal what the Holy Spirit has done in and through you.

Know that I am praying for you, Christ has prayed for you, and an army of women (earth-bound and heaven-found) are cheering for the One who will finish this race from within you. Christ is mighty in you. The Father is delighted in you. The Spirit is strong in your midst. I love you and I'm so proud of you!

TRUTHS

Jesus never asked you to go it alone. He never required that you tough it out and be independent.

Read Psalm 121:2 and describe where help comes from.

Where are some places you've looked for help in the past?

What would it tangibly look like for you to receive Jesus's help today as you run on mission?

QUESTIONS FOR REFLECTION

How do you feel different compared to when you started this study?

Did you have any misunderstandings about grace at the onset? If so, what were they?

Did you feel like a holy woman before? Is that how you'd identify now?

What did mission look like six sessions ago?

What will it look like moving forward?

What do you know about God that you didn't know then?

Spend some time praying and thanking Him for all that He's done.

WORSHIP WITH ME

Do me a favor, will you? Actually dance this week! Flip back to your favorite worship song or crank up one of these favorites of mine, but just do it. Dance this week because you have absolutely no reason not to!

- ✦ "Touch the Sky" by Hillsong United
- ✦ "Every Nation" by Lindy Conant

+ "Champion" by Brian and Katie Torwalt
+ "Set a Fire" by Will Reagan

READ

Before you celebrate, see this through to the end. Read *Dance, Stand, Run*, chapter 10. You already have everything you will ever need to run on mission, friend. Godspeed, and I'll see you on the course!

This was such a good idea. ☺

Dance, Stand, Run

The God-Inspired Moves of a Woman on Holy Ground

Jess Connolly

Grace is always good news. But it's not cheap—true grace compels us to change. That's where holiness comes in.

Beloved writer, speaker, and bestselling coauthor of *Wild and Free*, Jess Connolly will be the first to admit that not long ago, like many women, she grasped grace but she had forgotten holiness. *Dance, Stand, Run* charts her discovery that holiness was never meant to be a shaming reminder of what we "should" be doing, but rather a profound privilege of becoming more like Christ. That's when we start to change the world, rather than being changed by it.

Dance, Stand, Run is an invitation to the daughters of God to step into the movements of abundant life: dancing in grace, standing firm in holiness, and running on mission. Through story and study, Jess casts a fresh vision for how to live into your identity as a holy daughter of God, how to break free of cheap grace and empty rule-keeping, and finally, how to live out your holy influence with confidence before a watching world. Spoiler alert: it's a beautiful thing.

For anyone longing to take their place in what God is doing in the world, *Dance, Stand, Run* will rally your strength, refresh your purpose, and energize your faith in a God who calls us to be like Him.

Available in stores and online!